Facebook for Business: How to Use Facebook Ads to Find Your Target Audience and Increase Revenue

AARON C. ST. HILAIRE

ISBN: 0-692-93644-0
ISBN-13: 978-0-692-93644-3

CONTENTS

The Basics

Introduction to Facebook Advertising

Now you're probably thinking, "Why do I need an introduction to Facebook ads? I wouldn't be here if I didn't already know what they were." Well, arguably the most important thing that everyone needs to know about studying any subject is the fundamentals. I'd be doing you a major disservice if I jumped straight into the advanced tactics before establishing the basics. This applies to anything in life, in order to be successful at anything, it's extremely lucrative that you lay the groundwork before stacking your building blocks. Facebook ads are no different. If you've never run a Facebook ad campaign before this will all be new to you. That's actually a good thing, it means that you're not coming into this with any bad habits. If you are currently running Facebook ads with little success, we're going to fix that.

Facebook can play an important role in marketing your business through connecting and building key relationships with the audience that is interested in what you have to offer. Worldwide, there are over 1 billion monthly active Facebook users and it continues to grow. On average, Facebook advertising reaches 89% of its anticipated audience. That essentially means that 9 times out of 10, you are hitting the anticipated audience that you were looking to target, your target audience. To put it into perspective, imagine putting your money into a stock and having an 89% success rate or winning 89% of your poker hands. That's the type of high success rate you can have with Facebook. With their tools for businesses, you have the ability to create your ads and set your budget so that they reach all the right people in your target market at the price you expect to pay, 100% of the time.

The whole point of utilizing the Facebook ads platform is for YOUR own benefit. The benefits it adds to your business and marketing, to name a few, are: increased traffic to your offer, make more sales, build your email and customer list, growing your social media outreach, getting more followers, and building relationships and trust with your target market. All of these things are important in business. All of these things can be accomplished with Facebook.

You have the ability to create multiple ads to help build your audience, it's not just a one and done. You can have many different ad objectives and many variations of your ads sent out to a variety of audiences. It's amazing how specifying your targeting options enables you to show your ads to all of the people that you want to reach. It doesn't matter if you want to target just one audience or ten, you can do so with all these different targeting options. Facebook provides those tools to help you budget your ad spending and track your ads to see which versions work best. It's not just one at a time you can have twenty ads running at the same time and be able to see which ones are working best for you.

So why Facebook ads? You will learn: what the different types of ads are, all the features of an ad, the different ways you can target your audience. You'll also learn how to track your budget and the different payment structures available. We're going to get into advanced segmentation, different ways that I've used ads to accomplish different sales, and tons more so if you're ready.

Let's Get Started

This section is specifically written for someone who does NOT have a Facebook ads account. If you do have an ads account, you can move on to *choosing your objective*. We're going to do a quick run through in order to understand how to go about creating an ad. Firstly, setting up your account is very easy. If you already have a Facebook account/profile, all you would need to do is go to *business.facebook.com* and sign up for a business manager account. To start, make sure you've gathered all the information you need for your ad. You'll need your website URL, the specific goal for each campaign, and the budget for the campaign and delivery. You will also need the time, date, and place if relevant, and a photo to include in the ad. You're then going to choose an objective, which we'll cover in the next section. Next, you'll need your ad text and images. Finally, you'll choose your audience and budget which we will look at closer shortly.

Here is a pictorial review:
If you login to your normal Facebook account and look on the left-hand side of your profile you'll see two options here create page and create ad (this may change over time).

CREATE
Ad · Page · Group · Event ·
Fundraiser

When you click on *create page*, you are given the option to create a fan page which you need in order to create business manager account. When you're ready, create a business manager account, which you'll need in order to create ads. Go to *business.facebook.com* and select *create account*.

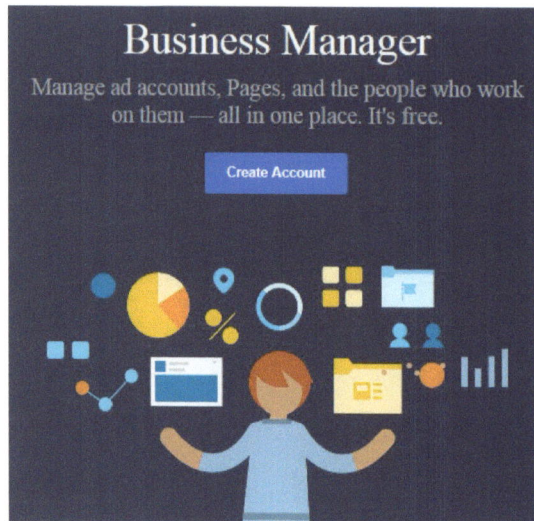

From there you will be taken through a set of options in order to sign up. Once you go through the settings for the business manager account, it'll ask for your fan page, business information, and payment information. If you are approved for the business manager account, you'll be able to work on your first ad.

Now that you have an account, for simplicity, go back to your normal Facebook profile and instead of clicking on *create page*, this time you'll select *create ad*. The basic ad manager will open up and should look something like this.

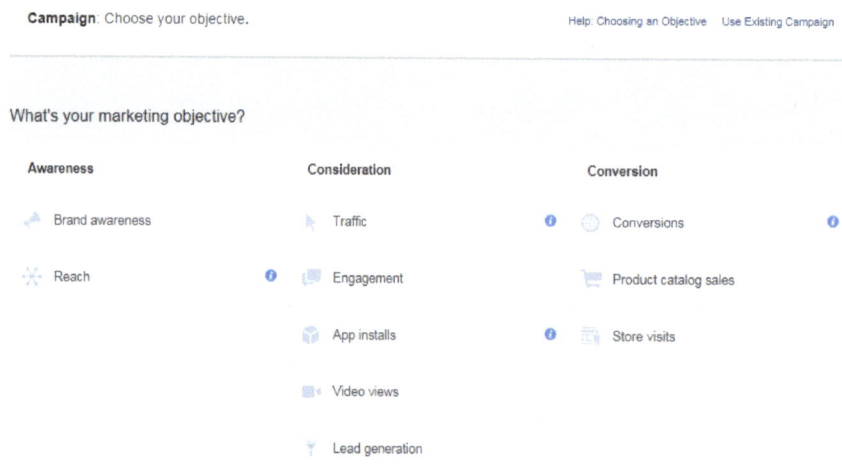

10

Let's say you want to run traffic to your website, you'll simply click on *traffic*, enter a campaign name, I'll leave it as "Traffic," and click continue.

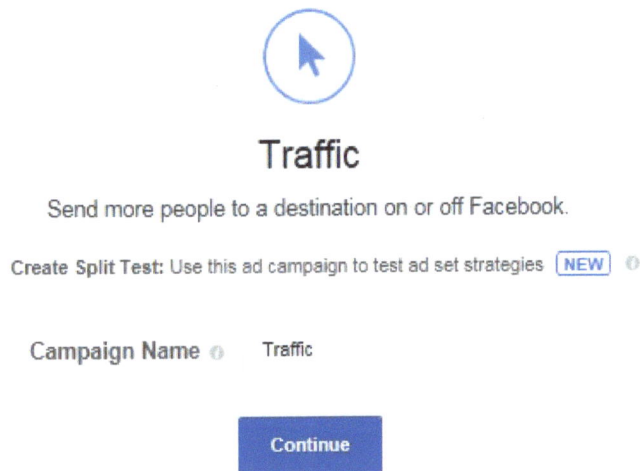

Traffic

Send more people to a destination on or off Facebook.

Create Split Test: Use this ad campaign to test ad set strategies [NEW] ⓘ

Campaign Name ⓘ   Traffic

[Continue]

Now that we've chosen the objective, we can label our ad set by specific name. This is called a naming convention. Use it so that you're able to determine the different ad set names for reference later.

Ad Set Name ⓘ   Put Something Unique Here

Next, we're going to create our audience. Here is all the audience information mentioned earlier from location, to custom audiences, to age, gender, language, etc.

Audience
Define who you want to see your ads. Learn more.

Create New   Use a Saved Audience ▼

Custom Audiences ⓘ   [Add Custom Audiences or Lookalike Audiences]

Exclude   Create New ▼

Locations ⓘ   Everyone in this location ▼

United States   ⌃
⦿ **United States**   ⌄

⦿ Include ▼ | Type to add more locations | Browse

Add Bulk Locations...

Age ⓘ   18 ▼   -   65+ ▼

Gender ⓘ   **All**   Men   Women

Languages ⓘ   [Enter a language]

Detailed Targeting ⓘ   INCLUDE people who match at least ONE of the following ⓘ

[Add demographics, interests or behaviors]   Suggestions | Browse

Exclude People

Connections ⓘ   Add a connection type ▼

Save This Audience

Remember, this is the main ad manager. Throughout this book we're going to be creating our ads in the Power Editor, which is a tool that gives you the ability to create multiple ads at once and gives you more precise control over your campaigns. This is better than the basic ad manager for when we get into more advanced segmentation for your ads.

To continue with this exercise, you fill in all your details based on the audience you're looking to target and you can save this audience for future use. Later in this book, we'll be going over audience research which can take hours and may be complex depending on how much research you do, so saving your audience will save you hours of having to research all over again.

You then with set up your placements, budget, whether it's daily or lifetime, the start and end date, any advanced options you may want for your ad, whether it's the optimization, the pricing, if you want to set your bid amount, when you plan to run your ads, etc. We'll talk about each of those more in the meat of the book.

Placements
Show your ads to the right people in the right places.

- **Automatic Placements (Recommended)**
  Your ads will automatically be shown to your audience in the places they're likely to perform best. For this objective, placements may include Facebook, Instagram and Audience Network. Learn more.

○ **Edit Placements**
  Removing placements may reduce the number of people you reach and may make it less likely that you'll meet your goals. Learn more.

Budget & Schedule
Define how much you'd like to spend, and when you'd like your ads to appear. Learn more

Budget ⓘ	Daily Budget ▼	$20.00
		$20.00 USD

Actual amount spent daily may vary. ⓘ

Schedule ⓘ
- Run my ad set continuously starting today

Set a start and end date

You'll spend no more than **$140.00** per week.

Optimization for Ad Delivery ⓘ — Link Clicks ▼

Bid Amount ⓘ
- **Automatic** - Let Facebook set the bid that helps you get the most link clicks at the best price.

  Manual - Enter a bid based on what link clicks are worth to you.

When You Get Charged ⓘ
Link Click (CPC)
More Options

Ad Scheduling ⓘ
Run ads all the time
More Options

Delivery Type ⓘ
Standard - Show your ads throughout your selected schedule (recommended)
More Options

Hide Advanced Options

After that, you can go ahead and click continue and you've completed the creation of your ad set. Within your ad set, you can now create your ad, so again we'll give this ad a specific name here.

Ad Name ⓘ   Cool Ad Name

Then, you can choose between creating a new ad or using an existing post on your Facebook fan page. For the sake of this demonstration, we're going to create a new ad. Next, select the Facebook fan page to connect to, this is the page you created earlier in this section. Also, if you have an Instagram account, you can link that here as well, if you plan on utilizing ad placement on Instagram.

Create New Ad   Use Existing Post

Pages

Connect Facebook Page
Your business is represented in ads by its Facebook Page.

Aaron St. Hilaire   ▼   +

or Turn Off News Feed Ads

Instagram Account
This Facebook Page will represent your business in Instagram ads, or you can add an Instagram account. ⓘ

Aaron St. Hilaire (Page) ✔   OR   ⊙ Add an Account

Moving into formatting for your ad, you can choose from a carousel of two or more images, a single image, a single video, a slideshow, or a collection. There is also an option to create a full screen experience. This is, for example, instead of someone leaving Facebook to go to your website or landing page, the contents of that page actually opens up in Facebook once they click on your ad. This enhances the user experience.

From here you can upload up to six images or you can browse the free Shutterstock options.

To wrap up your ad creation, we are going to input our website URL, since we're driving traffic to our website. After that, we can input our headline, ad copy, and call to action. There are also advanced options such as a newsfeed link, if you'd like to track a conversion pixel, etc.

Links
Enter the text for your ad. Learn more

Destination

WEBSITE

- Website URL

  http://www.example.com/page

MESSENGER

Message Text

Structured Message (JSON)

Headline

Text

Enter text that clearly tells people about what you're promoting

Call To Action (optional)

Learn More ▾

Show Advanced Options -

You can select any of the various options to preview what your ad is going to look like when it specifically placed on the following: mobile news feed, right hand column, desktop news feed, instant articles etc.

Ad Preview

Mobile News Feed ▾

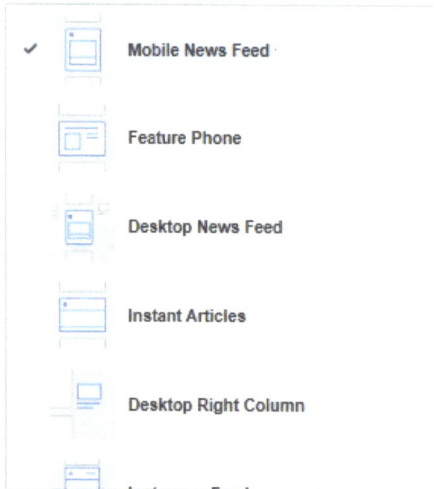

✓ Mobile News Feed

Feature Phone

Desktop News Feed

Instant Articles

Desktop Right Column

Once you're satisfied, you can select place order and you're good to go.

Choosing your Marketing Objective

Choosing your objective is particularly important because by choosing the correct objective for your ad, you're able to get the best possible ad type to deliver the results that you expect and need. What are Facebook ad objectives? Facebook lets you choose the placement of your ad and the ads of objective as you can see in Figure ().

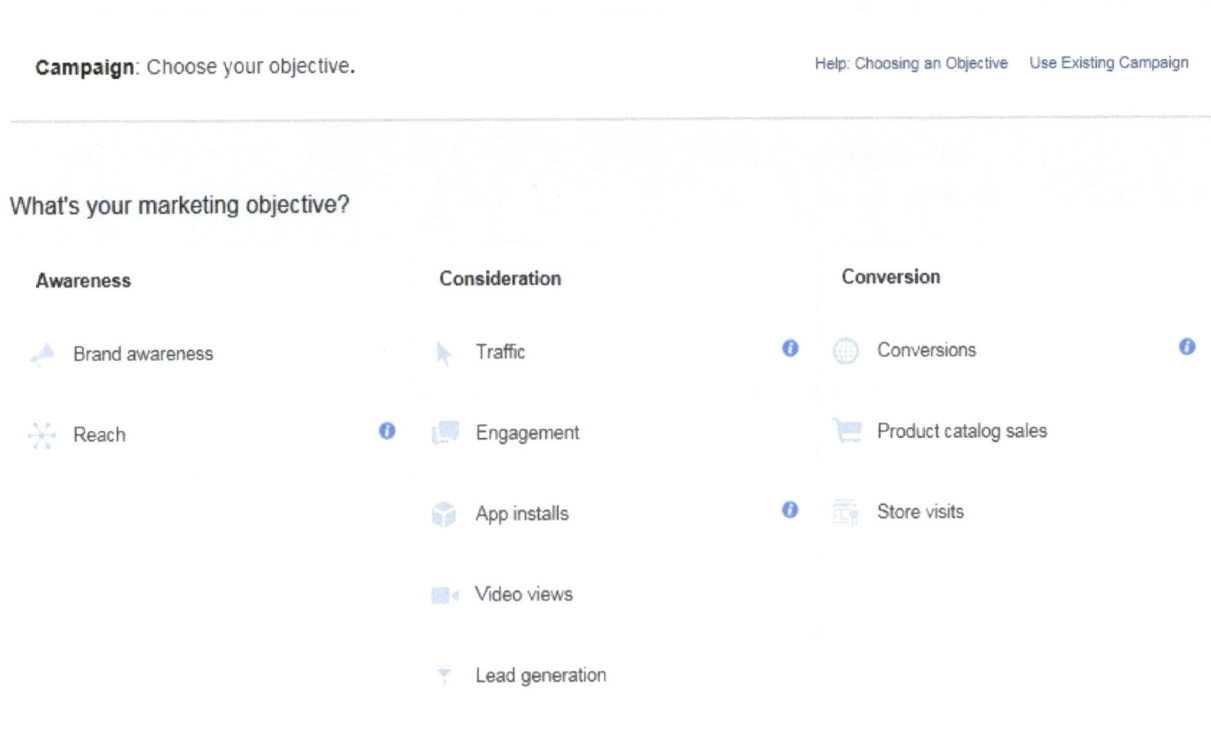

Campaign: Choose your objective.   Help: Choosing an Objective   Use Existing Campaign

What's your marketing objective?

Awareness	Consideration	Conversion
Brand awareness	Traffic	Conversions
Reach	Engagement	Product catalog sales
	App installs	Store visits
	Video views	
	Lead generation	

There all sorts of ad objectives such as: page post engagement, page likes, clicks to website, website conversion, etc. For instance, if your objective is to get more likes, you'll get more likes. If your intention is to get more clicks to your website, that's exactly what you will receive. Each ad objective will produce different results. You can also use multiple ad objectives to get different results. For example, you can still use the clicks to website objective to get conversions, it's all about being able to understand what each objective means to you.

With page post engagement, you're creating ads that boosts your posts. Meaning, increasing likes, shares, video plays, and photos views on posts you want more engagement on. With a website conversion objective, you're promoting a specific action that you want people to take such as opting-in for an eBook or signing up via email for a video series. Similarly, app installs encourage your audience to install an app from Facebook and app engagement gets you more activity for your app. Local awareness ads encourage locals to become prospective buyers, whether it's contacting you or getting driving directions to your location. Event responses for all intents and purposes increase the attendance to your Facebook page event. Pretty simple to understand, right? It's basically choosing the one that fits your needs.

When setting up your ad, you have the option of using an existing post from the drop-down menu. This works well if you're very active on your Facebook page, you're able to choose a past post or existing post and turn it into an ad. You can also create what is known as a dark post. A dark post is an ad that you create that does not show up on your timeline or newsfeed. With dark posts, the only people who see them are the ones that you target. Before you've created an ad and are ready to publish, ALWAYS, ALWAYS, ALWAYS preview your ad. Be sure to click on the different views to see it in a mobile setting, desktop setting, right hand column setting, etc. Facebook ads appear differently depending on the device the end-user is using to view Facebook in that specific location. If you're not careful, it can interfere with your results and ultimately increase your ad spend. Everything is different depending on the device. Your image might look crisp and clean on desktop and sometimes it may look horrendous on mobile, so make sure you check your ad images when running them to multiple devices.

Let's look at the page likes objective. This ad format helps you get new fans to your page. Your page will come up in the news feed whether it's mobile, desktop, or show up in the right-hand side, telling people to like your page based on their interests. It's simply getting people to agree that they like the content you're posting.

The website conversion objective requires you to place a conversion pixel on your website. A conversion pixel is literally a little pixel that cookies and tracks visitors that have come to your website. It can track their activity whether they visited your landing page and didn't opt-in with their phone number or email address. Maybe they did opt-in and was directed the next page in your funnel, but did not proceed to the checkout page. In this example, you can create a custom audience to target the people that hadn't proceeded to the checkout page with a different or even an email follow-up. Something like, "We noticed you were interested in learning more about our product, but didn't finish watching the presentation. Here's a link to continue where you left off." This brings back someone that may have been interested but left the page because something else grabbed their attention. Utilizing a pixel on all of your pages is extremely important because you want to track that kind of activity.

Ad Format

It is possible to publish a text-only ad; however, it is less effective than using a photo or video. However, if you do choose to create a text-only ad, Facebook recommends 90 characters or less. I believe in storytelling because people are typically more interested in a story rather than a pitch, so I recommend if you're doing text-only it better be a long-form story. Adding a picture or video makes it way more effective though.

As for text on images, images can contain no more than 20% text. Yes, you can you get an ad approved with more than 20% text, but going against the rules of Facebook can be costly. For image selection, you can choose page photos, previous ad images, upload new images, or choose from a selection of Shutterstock photos at no extra cost. The best size image upload is 1200 x 628 pixels. Facebook recommends a minimum width of 600 pixels for images appearing in the news feed. If you create your image to be 1200 x 628, it does resize perfectly for mobile, the feed on the right-hand side, and other formats.

In regards to videos, in the ads create tool you can choose your ad objective and what you want to advertise. Simply just click on the upload new video or browse library, to upload your video. Then you just fill in the text and links you want in the ad, very simple. If you decide to do a video views campaign, a clicks to website, or website conversions campaign, you can upload videos and all you have to do is upload a new video or choose one from your library.

Facebook's app install, website conversions, and click the website ad objectives, all ask for a call-to-action. Simply choose the type of action you want people to take or choose, no button. They've been adding more options when it comes to call-to-actions. Here are a few: no button, shop now, book now, learn more, sign up, download, they've even added contact us, and they're going to be adding more calls-to-action over time. It's your choice whether or not you want to choose these calls to action, you don't have to at all it's just there for your own selection.

Targeting Perspectives

Again, early on here we're going to be going over the basics. We'll go over advanced targeting strategies in a later section, but these strategies are essential when it comes to creating your first ad.

Targeting specific groups of people will help you get your ad in front of the people most likely to act on your ad. You can set your target audience in the ads create tool. You have plenty of options from: location, age range, gender, languages, interests, behaviors, connections, and custom audiences. When it comes to developing and putting your ads together to get them in front of the right people, it's extremely important you explore these options. The last thing you want to do is waste money advertising to people that are not likely to buy or test out your product or service.

Let's start with location. Here you can choose the cities, countries, and communities you want to target by entering city/town names, zip codes, you can even put in specific addresses. A really useful feature is the ability to set the radius for how far you want to expand when it comes to your location. With audience targeting you've got a lot of different options like interests, which is reaching people with certain interests, hobbies or pages they like on Facebook. Behaviors, which can be used to find people based on their purchasing behavior and device usage. You can even set a behavior for the car that someone drives. With connections, you reach people who are connected to your page, event, or app. You can create custom audiences using email addresses, phone numbers, and mobile advertiser IDs, however you cannot use IDs that have been scraped from anywhere in Facebook at all. That option is no longer allowed, don't do it. Targeting by location is also an option, you have the ability to target up to 25 countries per ad and you can target any combination of locations including: countries and cities, states and cities, cities and zip codes, two specific cities within a selected mile radius, etc. Age and gender targeting, allows you to choose the minimum and maximum age range of people who will consider your ad to be relevant and you'll typically choose both genders to send your ad to. Unless, your product is specifically for men or women. In terms of interest-based targeting you can browse the most popular categories and see the number of people who are interested in that category. You can also type in interest that you're looking for into the search bar and it will populate results very much like Google. If you're not quite sure the exact terminology you're looking for you can just start typing in an interest and Facebook will generate the specific terms. There are millions of additional attributes and suggestions based on the terms you enter and you can choose to target multiple categories or keywords from those interests. In behavior-based targeted, you can mix and match as well. For example, you can choose the categories of baseball and swimming and will reach anyone who likes either baseball or swimming, not just people who like both. With connection-targeting you can send an ad to people who are already connected to you on Facebook or not. You can also use it to show your ads to friends of people who have connected with you.

The more specific the details, the more effective your Facebook ad will be. That's the basics of targeting your audience on Facebook. Simply choose the connections that you want, choose the genders, choose the interest, a location, etc. The more specific it is to what you were looking for, the more targeted the group is.

Budgeting Perspectives

It may seem elementary but budgeting on Facebook is a bit different from regular budgeting. Everyone talks about Facebook's algorithm and the way you budget your campaign has an effect on how your ads are received by the end-user. Making sure that you put the proper budget in place so that your ads run efficiently and effectively is crucial. By setting up payment structures after you set your target audience you will have a better idea of how much your ads will cost. However, you should have a figure in mind before you begin setting up your payment structure and budget. You have to set your budget for your ad set and campaign from the get-go.

When you're putting together your ad set, there's going to be information on how much you want to spend per day or lifetime, for a budget, for that specific ad set. If you have five ad sets and you put $5 per day, that's $25 per day you plan on spending in your Facebook ads account. Begin by setting your country, your currency, and time zone if they're not already set. Your budget cost of advertising on Facebook really depends on the size of the audience and your budget. So, you can choose whether or not you want to budget at a set amount per day or set a lifetime budget. If you want to set up something 30 days within a specific budget you could actually set a lifetime budget of $1,000, for example, and schedule your ad out over the course of the 30 days and even during certain times of the day if you want to. You can choose to run your ad continuously starting that day or you can even select to start at a later date, at a specific time, and even choose when it ends, in the ad set schedule. In the pane on the right of your ad set setup you will get an estimated daily reach for the ads that you set up. If you set up an audience that has a million people it'll tell you how many people per day your estimated daily reach will be. After you've set your budget and schedule you will get an estimate of how much your ad will cost. The cost of your ads on Facebook is up to you, you may choose between a daily or lifetime budget, as well as cost per thousand impressions (CPM) or cost-per-click (CPC). When you're bidding on these ads, you pay for the impressions you receive based on the limit you set. After your ad has started to run, you have the ability to change the ad sets end date if needed. If the ad is set for lifetime budget it will automatically adjust to the remaining time left.

Facebook suggests you avoid frequent changes to the end date as it can interfere with their system's ability to optimize your ads. To be prepared, decide when you want your ad to end and leave it alone.

Once you set your budget, choose whether you want to pay per click or per impression. This determines how you will pay and who you will see your ad. With some campaigns, you want cost-per-click, with some you want cost per impressions, and it's truly dependent on your budget. With pricing, you have the choice of whether you want to automatically bid or manually bid for your ads. Automatic bidding is optimized by Facebook to reach your objective. Manual bidding allows you to pick the maximum bid, with a manual bid your ad will be optimized for clicks or impressions. However, it will not help you reach your objective. Consider that a very important point.

Finally, you'll want to set an account spend limit for your ad account because you never know when something may happen to your account. If you set a lifetime of $1,000 and it just so happens that your ad decides to take off in one day. Then you'll be fine because you set the limit. In the same scenario, if you never set the budget, it's just going to start spending a bunch of money because you never gave it a limit and it doesn't stop the account from spending. The account spend limit sets an overall limit for your entire ad account, if you only wanted to spend $1,000, you can actually have it stop at $1,000. This way all your ads in your account will stop running once it hits that amount. It's a good indication of how much is being spent and where your base lines are. To set up an ad account spend limit: in your ads manager go to billing, then go to manage under account spend, and set/update your limit.

Budget Tracking

If you care about your money, it's incredibly important to keep track of your advertising budget. Good marketing requires you stay on top of your marketing expenses. Billing can be accessed through your ads manager pane or in your business manager. The first time you create your ad spend limit, you won't have to worry about a minimum or maximum amount ever again because Facebook will automatically track it for you. When you update your account spend limit, you must set a limit less than 10% above the already set limit. Example, if it was $100, your limit can only be increased to $110. In the billing manager, you can find a detailed breakdown of your charges, containing everything from the amount you spent at that moment, the charge date, impression or click charges, etc. You can also create and export reports to see how well your ads are performing with the budget that is going in accordance with the ad. In order to get started, in the navigation menu of the ads manager, click on reports. Default data is for general metrics over the last 7 days for any active campaign and you can click on the blue export button to download the report. For your convenience, you could schedule reports to be delivered to your email automatically, all within the reporting dashboard of your ad manager.

Consider this frequently asked question. Why is the amount you spent different in your ads manager and the billing sections? The amount you spent might be different, since it appears as an estimate in your ads manager and your account spend limit, its takes up to 72 hours for your ad results to be fully processed, sometimes shorter. If you've reached a new billing threshold, your amounts will be different as well. You are only charged for what you actually spend. The billing summary amount will be the accurate final amount. Whatever Facebook charges you is the accurate amount that you spent. The reports give you estimates of what you spent at that moment, or the last couple days, or last month, etc. It even gives you an estimate into the future as to how much you will spend in your ads manager for that specific campaign. However, your most accurate amount is what's spent at that moment in time, based on what's been charged to your account. If you're advertising an external site or have chosen clicks as an objective, you're bidding on a cost-per-click basis. So, you won't be charged for your ad if it doesn't receive any clicks. Whether or not you have a billing threshold will determine how often you're charged for ads.

Power Editor

The majority of the advertising that I create on Facebook is done in Power Editor. Power Editor is a tool that helps businesses manage multiple campaigns, ad sets and ads. It's easy to create, edit, manage and optimize campaigns, ad sets, ads and Page posts in bulk, across a large number of different ad accounts and Pages. Power Editor allows you to create ads much more efficiently than if you did everything from the ads manager.

Inside of your ad account, in the top left you'll see the three-bar menu icon. When you click it, you should see an option that says power editor, if not when you hover over "all tools."

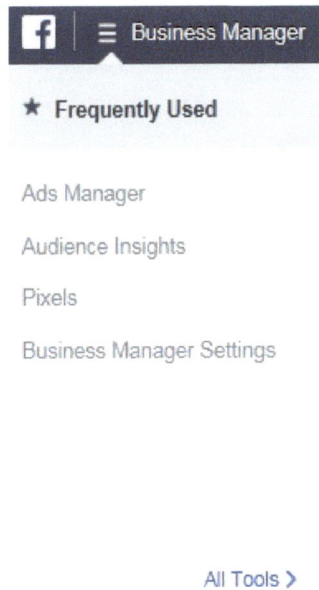

Under all tools, navigate your mouse to the "create & manage" column, you'll see Power Editor in that column.

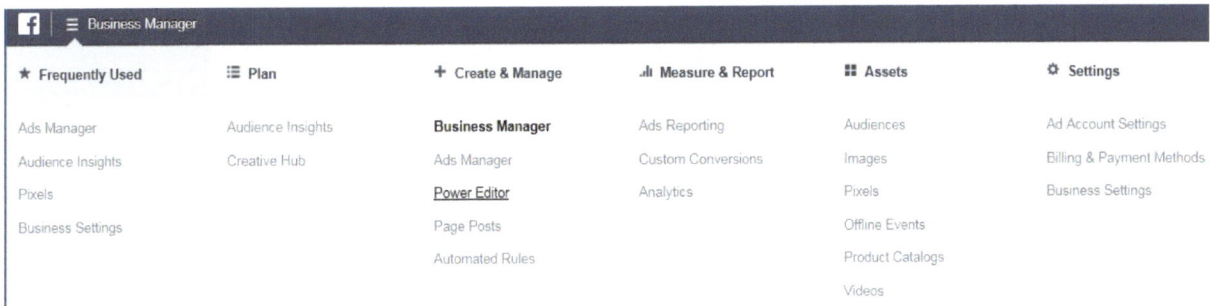

The Power Editor will showcase all the campaigns that you've created. This allows you to see all of your campaigns, ad sets, and all of your ads simultaneously. You could sort all of your ad sets as well as create multiple ad sets at any given time. Let's say we wanted to duplicate four ad sets at once: we'd simply highlight them, click duplicate, and then either create a new campaign or keep them within the same campaign. The point is that it's a lot more efficient to work inside of the Power Editor. When we're going to create an audience inside of the Power Editor, all we've got to do is click on the button that says create an ad set.

Campaigns | 1 selected ⊗ | ⊞ Ad Sets for 1 Campaign | ▢ Ads for 1 Campaign

+ Create Ad Set ▾ | ⊞ Duplicate ▾ | ✎ Edit | Quick Edits ▾ | ↻ | 🗑 | ⚌ | ↩ | 🖺 | Create Rule ▾

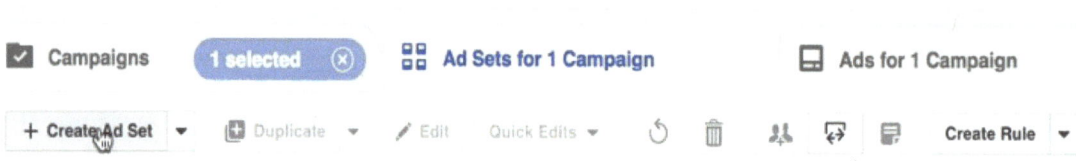

After that, simply select on the campaign and then label it. For example, we can label it test, select the objective, and click create.

Create Ad Set

Use Existing Campaign ⬍

Use Existing   Tony Robbins - Low cost countries   ✕

Create New Ad Set ⬍

Ad Set Name   Test

Skip Ad ⬍

Creating 1 ad set

Cancel   Create

What will happen in the power editor is all of the options will fill in from the get-go. Whereas in ad manager we would have to create the campaign step-by-step, which is great except it'll take a lot longer. We can then set our budget, the scheduling of when the ad goes out, our audience, etc. If you wanted to change the age, gender, language, and then expand upon the interest you would go ahead and do that. When you've completed all of your changes, simply click review changes and accept them. Facebook will automatically create your new campaigns, ad sets, or ads.

Discard Changes   ↑ **Review Changes (1)**

In summary, Power Editor is a time saver compared to the Ads Manager.

Understanding Facebook Ads

Five Mistakes to Avoid

There are five critical mistakes that most people make when running their ads and I want to make sure you are aware of them so you don't make these mistakes as well. Understand this, Facebook ads are a great way to get traffic, but you'll lose a lot of money if you're not clear with your objective. Do it right and you'll have floods of targeted traffic, really cheap, and you'll make higher margins of profit. Before you get started running ads; here are the five things you should never do when paying for your Facebook ad.

1. Don't ignore split testing. I don't know how often I see my clients or my students make this mistake. If you're not trying different ad variations, whether it's headlines, calls to action, images, etc. then you have no idea what works and what doesn't. That's not an effective way to do things. As marketers, we're always testing. It may seem confusing but there's a way to do it right and a way to do it wrong. Ignore this and your campaigns will be a complete waste of time and give you terrible results. I'll cover split-testing more thoroughly in a later section.

2. Don't target the wrong audience. This may seem obvious, but you'd be surprised how many people target audiences that have nothing to do with their product or service. If you are delivering something to a real estate niche, specifically investors, and you are targeting real estate in general; people looking to buy and sell homes, not just investors, then it's too broad and you're targeting a lot of people who don't need your product or service. That's just one of the many examples that I see on a frequent basis. It's vital your ads are shown to the correct people. Your whole audience may not actually be a good fit for seeing your ads, so get the targeting just slightly wrong and your whole campaign will cost you much more than it should. Even worse, it will not convert. It happens, it's

unfortunate, the best of us sometimes make this mistake but it's something that you need to know.

3. Don't run ads to the devices that are not generating clicks or conversions. Certain ad types and devices are driving the bulk of your traffic, you'd probably be surprised once you check your reports. Adjust them to reflect which devices are generating the traffic conversions. When you run ads, always check your reports to see if it's desktop or mobile. If it is mobile ads, you can further break down your audience by seeing which devices are generating the clicks, leads, and conversions. It's important to do because it grants you the ability to see what is getting you the best return on investment. It doesn't make any sense to run ads to devices that are doing nothing for you. That's just wasting money. Of course, you need to run ads for some time in order to get that data, but don't leave it on if it's not doing anything for you. Don't start big and throw lots of money away. There's no way cleverer than to start small and make every dime count. That way, no money is wasted. Be smart.

4. Don't start with a big budget. It's more efficient to start with $5/day, $10/day, on the per ad set level. This allows you to gather data on a small scale so you can make better decisions of what to do with your ad campaign down the road. When running ads at $5 to $10/day for 2 to 3 days you'll gather enough information to know whether or not a campaign is going to work on the upper ad set level. If all of your ad sets are underperforming, let's say you have five ads running at $5/day. Then you spend $50 to $100 and you see nothing's happening. That's a sign that maybe you need to try something else and the same concept applies when you're testing devices. You have to test everything. Don't start too large and throw away your money, don't go after interests with 4 million people in it, and spend $5 because you're not really going to get a

big enough sample size. Start small and use a little bit of money here and there until you find the right mix of people.

5. Don't send your traffic to inconsistent content or an inconsistent offer. By inconsistent, I mean, don't send your traffic to a page that doesn't connect with the ad, people will just bounce. Bouncing is a term that represents the percentage of visitors who enter the site and then leave, "bounce", rather than continuing on to view other pages within the same site. If they bounce, your money and traffic is wasted. If you're talking about something in related to fishing and then you send them to a page that's all about why you need to do check out some water activities, it makes no sense, it's an inconsistent offer. Make sure that you are providing the audience with an ad and an image that correlates with your product or service.

Compliance and TOS

Many people make the mistake of not reading the compliance in the terms of Facebook advertising and they get their account shut down or get their ads constantly disapproved. My goal is to share with you what I have learned from my own experience and the experiences of others, what to do for the sake of compliance when it comes to Facebook ads. This is probably one of the best messages you can ever receive from the compliance team: "given your commitment and understanding to making the community experience better, we feel comfortable enabling the ad accounts that were disabled." If your account was disabled, wouldn't you love to see this response? It's not often that people see this response from Facebook support, so I'm going to walk you through some things that I've learned in regards to what Facebook uses to determine certain things when it comes to ads, what Facebook uses to measure the credibility of websites, simply following compliance.

Facebook uses this website called Web of Trust which is a scoring system used for URL blacklisting. You can go to mywot.com to learn more about Web of Trust. Before ever checking your landing page, ad copy, ad image, or targeting; their first checking to see what other people think about you, people can go on this site and rate your website based off of their experiences being on the site. This tool shows an icon next to every link in browsers, any browser, in email, and even in your Facebook news feed. You'll see a green, yellow, or red circle next to each link. If your green rating turns into orange, yellow, or red; that means anyone clicking from Facebook to your URL gets an automatic warning before being redirected.

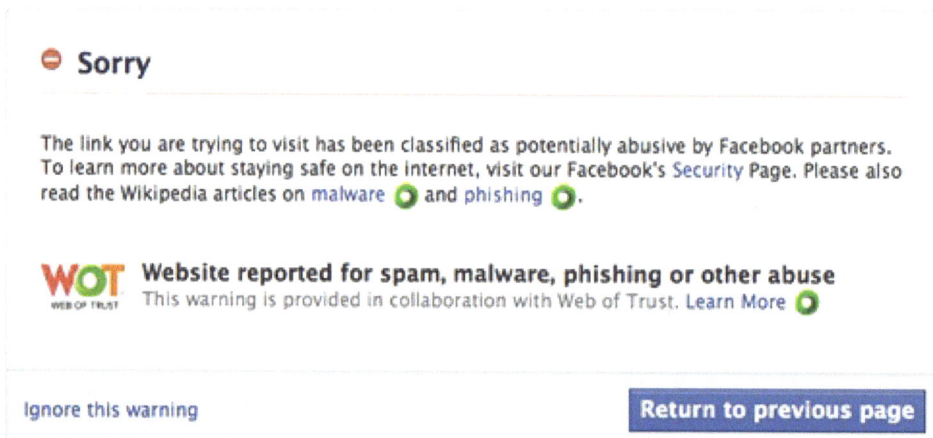

If you have a negative rating for any reason this is the default warning that is displayed. Can you imagine someone clicking your link and this pops up? What are the chances that they're going to go to your site? Be very careful with what you put on your website, whether or not your images are consistent with the context of your site, because if what you are delivering from the ad image and the ad copy doesn't match with what's on your site, people can say that your site is deceptive and that can get it a red dot rating from Web of Trust.

If you do have issues with your account you can email ad support with all compliance and business manager questions. There are two departments there's Global Marketing which is for Facebook ad Educators, then there's policy which is for the ad enforcers. The policy department does the account terminations and the Global Marketing team tries to avoid all the account terminations. If you feel that your account is wrongfully terminated or ads wrongfully disapproved, you should go to facebook.com/business/resources. Replying to any ad account termination emails or contacting Facebook through their in-line termination message, goes to the policy team, and they aren't responsible for helping you get your account back. You must get in touch with the Global Marketing team if you need help.

When contacting Facebook don't be nasty. Be nice use language they want to hear like, "I'm a good advertising citizen," which I've heard from countless people is what they request that you say. Also, record short videos anytime you are messaging them. Do not write out the entire problem in text, a short one to three-minute video explaining the issue has a bigger impact.

All agencies or businesses need to use the business manager, it should be very obvious by now. You can set up new accounts for clients inside your business manager and you can even set up multiple accounts for yourself inside of your own business manager. This is where they want you running your ads as a business. It helps explain why there are multiples logins into your account. Whether it's from employees or any contractors. You also want to use a business email account, they want to see real businesses on board. Marketers and advertisers need to stop trying to game the system if we expect to have Facebooks support and communication. It's as simple as that, don't try to be sketchy.

Facebook strongly believes that advertising can improve the Facebook user experience. Facebook has no issue with direct response or affiliate marketers. The only issue is proving that what you are advertising can improve the user experience. A lot of affiliates are just trying to make a quick buck they're not really providing anything of value and Facebook is looking for people who are looking to enhance the user experience. If that's you, ask yourself, would "blank" think this campaign improves the Facebook's user experience or detracts from it? Ask yourself that before putting up a campaign. Trust is most important to the policy team, so don't use images that have nothing to do with the offer or ad copy. Don't create ads that use fear or hype. Don't create landing pages that don't disclose the business model and don't create videos with no player controls or force the user to wait. This is very unconventional for a lot of people in the marketing space.

In the advertising space, these are all tactical ways that you're able to clicks, but Facebook does not want that. They want content that enhances every user, with their experience. You have to be careful with what you post. When a user exits out your ad or requests to hide them, they use that as a signal to investigate your account. If they get complaints but your ads aren't misleading, your landing pages clearly disclose your business model, you're not doing anything wrong, trying to trick, deceive, or frustrate any users, your fine. It's okay to remove nasty or spammy comments, but deleting all negative responses is frowned upon. Not everything that comes up negative from a user is a bad thing, you could always reply to those comments in a way that makes you look like the "bigger person." You simply have to leave some of these responses on the ad or on your page so that it looks more natural, no business is perfect.

A lot of marketers and advertisers are running video sales letters and squeeze pages with their ads and Facebook is okay with list building and sales videos. They are not okay with list building pages that do not clearly identify the business and business model. That is what they're looking for. Go read the terms of service and page guidelines, follow them, they're constantly being updated. You need to be aware of what's going on in Facebook. Also, in your audiences, delete any UID campaigns you may have run in the past and clean out any ads or pages that are against TOS. If there's anything that you've done in the past that you think is borderline red flag to Facebook, just delete it, you don't need those campaigns.

You can view all the policies for advertised products and services here: www.facebook.com/help/399392800124391

Page guidelines can be seen here: www.facebook.com/page_guidelines.php

Make sure you follow all of these compliance guidelines when it comes to your Facebook ads. You can review any new compliance added to these policy pages. Make sure that you are constantly up-to-date with them. I personally check it once a week just to make sure nothing has been added. If you keep up with all policies, terms, and conditions with Facebook, your account will not get shut down.

Positive and Negative Feedback

There is a feature that allows you to figure out what is considered positive and what is considered negative to the people you're targeting with your ads. One of the most popular ways I see Facebook advertisers getting their accounts banned is by not watching their negative feedback. Here is how you monitor and edit ads based on feedback.

In order to find the positive and negative feedback, navigate to your ads manager. Open up a campaign, then go into the ad set, and select one of your ads. Let's look at one of my ads.

Ad Name	Relevance ... ⓘ	Positive Fee... ⓘ	Negative Fee.. ⓘ
Fast Cars Club - Video vi...	10	High	Medium

You can see here that the relevant score on this ad is 10/10, the positive feedback is high, and the negative feedback is medium. Although, this ad has been successful and cheap, it could be even better and even cheaper if the negative feedback was in the ideal range, low. Essentially, the perfect line-up would be a relevance score of 10, a high positive feedback and a low negative feedback. The positive feedback is an estimated score based on the number of times people are expected to interact with your ad (example: reacting to a post, clicking a link) and help you achieve your objective. The negative feedback is a score based on the number of times people hid your ad or chose not to see ads from you. I recommend you look at the feedback for each and every one of your ads.

If you want to check all of your ads' feedback at once use the same process above and simply select all of your ads. To make it easier, click the columns drop-down and select customize columns...

Columns: Performance ▾

✓ **Performance (Default)**

Delivery

Engagement

Video Engagement

App Engagement

Carousel Engagement

Performance and Clicks

Cross-Device

Messenger Engagement

Offline Conversions

Customize Columns...

Set as Default

Reset Column Widths

From there you can deselect all of the options on the right-hand side of the screen and then select: relevance score, positive feedback, and negative feedback, then click apply.

Customize Columns

Performance

Engagement
Page Post
Messaging
Media
Clicks
Awareness

Conversions
Website
Apps
On Facebook
Offline
Store Visits

Settings

Search ×   Clear Search   4 COLUMNS SELECTED

PERFORMANCE   Select All Colu   Ad Name

Results   Relevance Score ×
Result Rate   Positive Feedback ×
Reach   Negative Feedback ×
Frequency
Impressions
Delivery
Social Reach
Social Impressions
Actions
People Taking Action
✓ Relevance Score
✓ Positive Feedback
✓ Negative Feedback
Amount Spent
Amount Spent Today

ATTRIBUTION WINDOW
28-day click and 1-day view
Comparing Windows

Save as preset   Cancel   Apply

Once you've done that, you can view all of the positive and negative feedback from all of your ads. For the ones with high negative feedback, you can either turn them off or adjust the copy and/or images and test it out again. The goal here is to be sure that your audience is actually interested in your ad.

Compliant Landing Pages

This information goes side-by-side with the compliance and terms of service. For compliant landing pages, the destination you're running your ad to must function properly in all browsers: Chrome, Firefox, Internet Explorer, Safari, Opera, etc. The Facebook team reviews landing pages from a variety of international locations. Therefore, if you are advertising an external website that is restricted to people in certain regions your ad may be disapproved. It's strange, you would think by blocking out certain countries, if you don't have a history of getting buyers in certain regions, that you'd be saving yourself some headaches and money. However, it may actually get your ads disapproved.

Ads may not direct to landing pages that trigger pop-ups or pop-unders. A lot of the people typically use pop-ups or pop-unders to attract the visitors that may have considered leaving the site at first. Then, they decided to take a chance because they had a secondary message pop up in their window, asking them to leave their email, etc. Unfortunately, Facebook does not like that, so turn off pop ups and pop-unders, at least from your landing pages. Some of these pop-ups tend to look spammy and users find it to be annoying. Facebook doesn't want you to manipulate the end user's behavior or get them to do something they wouldn't normally do, it's invasive. Also, landing pages must clearly and accurately reflect the product or service being promoted in your ad. Do not mislead the user, you can read more about this on the ad guidelines provided by Facebook.

Have you seen those pages where as soon as the website loads, a video starts playing? Those are not allowed. Also, if your landing page does have a video, you cannot turn off the controls, the ones that let the users: rewind, fast forward, pause, or play. Remember, we're talking about your landing page. If you're landing page consists of a form or something simple like that, you can then have an auto-play video with no controls, on the next page in your funnel, if you'd like. Another thing Facebook requires you to have is a privacy policy, terms of service, and other applicable legal information (earnings disclaimer), easily accessible for the user to access. The typical placement for these links are in the footer of your landing page. The user must also be able to easily identify whom they're working with and/or doing business with. You should add contact information such as: phone number, email address, and mailing address to your landing page.

Also, no outrageous claims or claims you can't prove on your ads, no fear based ads and/or super hyped angles. Ad copy must describe and represent the sponsored brand or product in an accurate and non-misleading way. Ads must not make unsubstantiated claims including but not limited to: price, performance, and results. Any claim made in the copy, should also be reflected on the landing page. Be clear on what your landing page is providing for the user, the bait-and-switch tactic is not allowed.

For the sake of your account, it's incredibly important that you know all of these restrictions. Facebook has specific guidelines, for its ads, for certain industries as well. In the fitness industry for example, certain types of body based images that has to do with weight loss can't be run. If you're in the medical industry, you have to be careful of your customer's privacy. If you're in the software industry, you can't trigger automatic downloads, spyware, tracking devices or any other software that go into the user's computer, without their consent or prior knowledge. The same restrictions of content that is banned by Facebook are the same restrictions that apply to your landing pages. Consider all of these terms, conditions, restrictions, and compliance provided by Facebook when creating landing pages to go along with your compliant advertising.

Retargeting

Retargeting is a critical aspect of putting together your ad campaign. Why? With retargeting, when a user visits your site and decides they're going to leave, you have the chance to grab their attention again as they browse other websites, your ad is actually placed on those web sites. When they go back to Facebook, your retargeted ad gets their attention again and brings them back to your site. That's the purpose of retargeting, to get them back in front of your offer, lead magnet, product, service, etc. It's simply reminding them, that this was something they were interested in but didn't follow through with the offer. Retarding is a part of your sales cycle, it's crucial, and you need to utilize it.

Retargeting ads get clicks to your offer or lead page. A retargeted ad can be a duplicate of the original ad, with a little twist. If you were selling products on Shopify and the user abandoned their cart, you're retargeting ad would say something like, "you forgot to check out," and provide them with a link to the item they had in their cart. This gives providers more ownership than paying for another visit from a brand-new customer. Picture this, 1,000 people come to your landing page and you have a custom audience pixel from Facebook on that page. Those 1,000 visits are going to be cookied, put into the pixel, and tracked by Facebook. Facebook will gather that information, show you that you've had 1,000 people visit your site, and you can now remarket or retarget them with a new or existing ad. That allows you to segment those lists and traffic, so that you can get them back to whatever it was you we're trying to sell them. You can give them a new message, offer, coupon, bonus, etc. Give them something that you think will attract them to come back to your service or product all over again.

Can you see how powerful that is? If you don't have retargeting setup for any of your campaigns, you are missing out on a huge percentage of traffic coming back to your site as well as a large percentage of potential sales.

There are two metrics you want to be sure to measure as well, cost per pixel and value per pixel. The cost per pixel is the media cost divided by the number of pixels (i.e. $500/2 pixels). Your value per pixel is the income generated divided by the number of pixels (you earn $500 with 2 pixels). Your media budget should be focused on driving targeted traffic to your content. Remember, Facebook is looking to enhance the user experience. Knowing that, you want to make sure anything that you promote to your audience is of high value to them and that you're driving them to the right type of content.

When a user visits your site, always have a retargeting pixel available. Even if you don't have retargeting ads at this moment, make sure you have that custom audience pixel on your website. Whether it's the homepage or it's URL specific, make sure that pixel is there. Use retargeting ads to show your offer or lead page. I want to make this very clear, you want to bring them back, that's the whole purpose.

Retargeting lists have multiple purposes. You can save on advertising costs, you can boost your conversions, you can promote tons of content to the same people who've already liked your content from the past, and your website because they've visited it before, and it also gives you additional branding; your face, your logo, shows up everywhere, over and over to these audiences. When we cover campaign set up, I'm going to show you exactly how-to set-up your retargeting ads. I want to make it very clear that you need this when you're developing your ad campaigns.

In summary, start using retargeting if you haven't already done so. Retarget on all channels available to you and all website URLs too. Finally, use retargeting to your advantage to get more sales and cheaper traffic back to your site. It's that simple set-up retargeting and benefit.

Audience Research

When it comes to who you're showing your ads to, audience research is the most important aspect of your campaign set-up. I actually recommend you research for at least three hours before you make any decisions. Granted, some industries may not require a ton of research. For example, if you're a real estate agent looking for people who are willing to sell their homes you can simply target homeowners who are likely to move, it may not be necessary to go much further than that. However, there are other industries where deeper research is required.

Your best friend in this process is going to be the audience insight tool. There are a bunch of ways you can go about researching your audience and I will go into more advanced options later. For now, I encourage you to play with the audience insight tool. Start by typing in one interest at a time and analyze your audience.

Let's say I'm a Pilates trainer and I'm trying to sell monthly membership for online Pilates classes. I'll open up my audience insight tool and type in Pilates in the interest section.

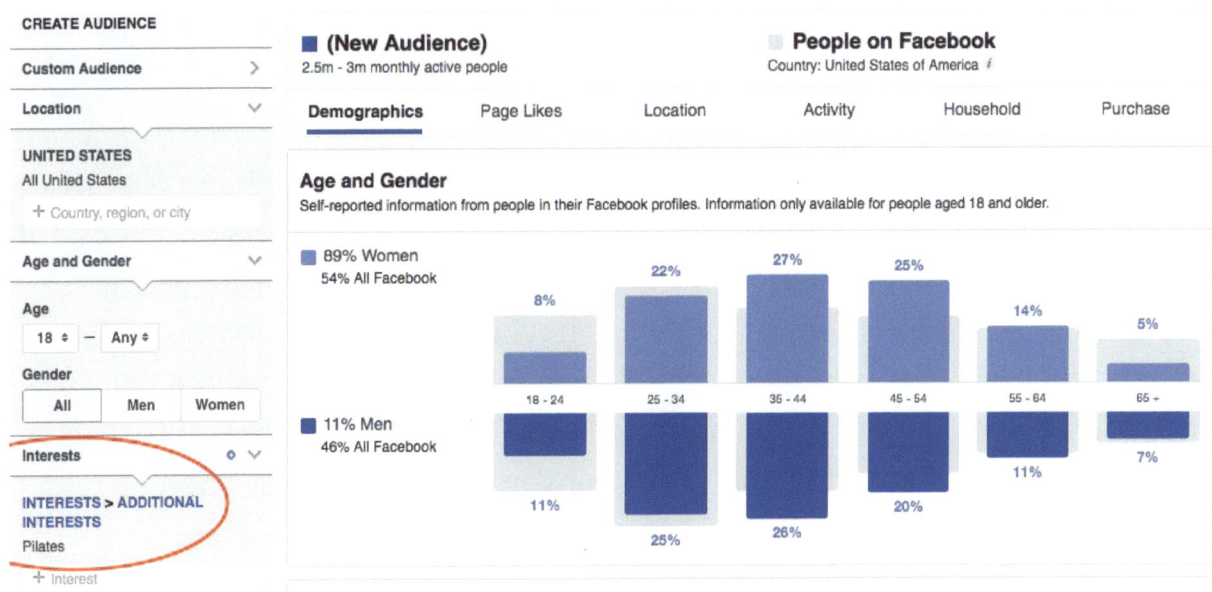

As you can see the Pilates audience in the United States has 2.5-3 million monthly active users and the majority almost 90% of that audience is women. Already, we've got some great information about our audience, we can also see that the bulk of the audience is between ages 25-64. That gives us a good starting point for our ads and gives us an idea of how to write the copy because we're going to be targeting women only. Let's also say that instead of online classes, we're going to be doing in-person classes in Miami. So, I'll use the information we've got to narrow down that audience to the Miami area.

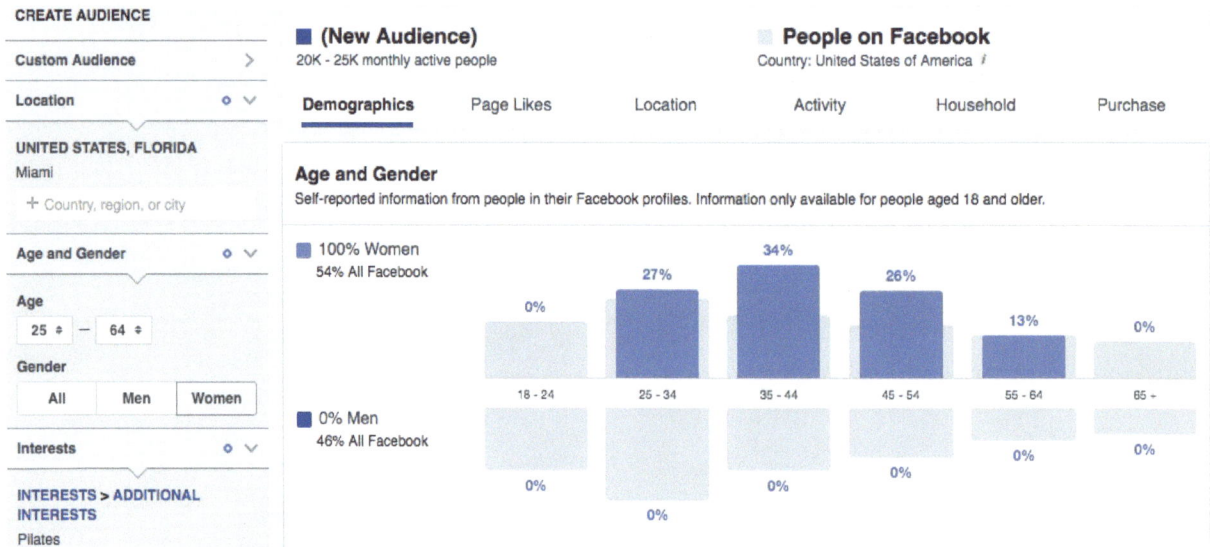

Now you can see we've made all of the changes above and have received an audience of 20-25 thousand monthly active users. This may be good for me to start testing and acquiring customers. Of course, if after testing and I found out it isn't working for me maybe I get more specific and target some more niched forms of Pilates, which I will talk about in advanced targeting. For now, the point is to test out different interests, audiences, behaviors, etc. The only way you're going to get good at targeting is by practicing.

If you're in a niche that's a little bit more difficult to target, it may be easier to search more in depth when you're in the "create ad" portion of ad manager. So just go to the ads manager, create an ad, pick an arbitrary objective, and you'll land on the ad set page. From there, you can scroll down to detailed targeting and start typing in the things you think may be good to target. I'll continue with the example of Pilates.

Notice how I've got an audience of 19,000,000 with just targeting Pilates and Facebook generates some niched interests within the Pilates realm like: Studio Pilates, Pilates Style, Physio Pilates, etc. These are where we can find the Pilates enthusiasts instead of targeting Pilates as a whole, so I'll select some of these and remove Pilates.

Now I've narrowed my audience down to 1.6 million of more niched Pilates interests. If I wanted to search further I can simply go to my normal Facebook account and in the search bar type in "pages related to Pilates", and you can do that for your niche as well.

Some new things came up that I didn't see Facebook recommend in the ads manager is Pop Pilates (my wife likes that page, that's pretty funny) and Peak Pilates, these are interests I can also use to target. I don't recommend running an ad with all of those interests at once though. You can use what you've learned about the power editor to create the same ad, just spread across each of the interests. That way, you will know which interests are actually generating leads and sales. The ones that aren't you can simply turn off. Again, it comes down to testing, you won't know which interests directly align with your offer unless you test them out.

There is way more to targeting than just interests. However, this should give you a great understanding before we go into more advanced targeting later. For now, I want you to play with some interests around your industry and keep an excel spreadsheet of potential interests. As long as your industry doesn't change you can save yourself the future hassle by saving a list of your go-to audiences.

Be prepared to test all of your interests. You will know the true winners once you start your testing.

Ad Psychology

Psychology of Ad Creation

Do you know what to incorporate in your ads in order to get clicks? When it comes to creating Facebook ad copy, I've used quite a few headline formulas that all work differently and have different purposes. Regardless of the amount of copy, people cling to a story. This is going to sound extremely elementary, but simple is good. When I say story, I mean beginning, middle, and end. The beginning refers to the "hook," something that grabs the viewers' attention, most of the time the hook will be a question.

Example (chiropractor): Do you suffer from lower back pain?

If you've got your targeting right, odds are they do suffer from lower back pain, so this will immediately capture their attention.

Moving onto the middle, express the conflict.

Meet Susie, when she came to me, she could barely walk. Her back would have her tossing and turning in her bed at night, she rarely got a full night's rest. Susie went to several specialists and their treatments just weren't working for her. When she came to my office, I knew exactly what the problem was. I told her that sometimes the stress is actually in the upper back and strings down so that the pain is only felt in the lower back. After the first round of treatment she started feeling less pain. After she came in for her second round of treatment, she reported the best night sleep that she's had in years.

The end will be you expressing how your product or service will solve that person's problem. In this sense...

If you're feeling like Susie use to, you're in luck, because right now you can download my free e-book that goes over effective self-remedies for lower back pain.

In this example, the landing page would capture the person's information so they can download the free book and maybe try to upsell an appointment after that.
Think of it like third grade: beginning, middle, end – or hook, conflict, solution.

You don't necessarily have to use all three in your ad copy but I'd at least use a hook and a solution.

People focus on benefits. When you speak to their pain point, they pay attention. They want to know how you can do something for them. The best ads I've ever created, with my network marketing company for example, generated a lot of traffic because people can relate to those pains: not making enough money, not having enough time freedom, not having time with their family, unable to have their dream job, there's a lot of ways it can be positioned. All you've got to do is tweak it for your product or service, what are the benefits? Write them down and use all of them! Speaking to that pain point can sometimes be the most powerful thing that you can put into your ad copy.

There's plenty of way you can go about this. Tired of brittle dry hair? Our natural treatment will make your hair shiny and strong, shampoo ad. That's the type of thing that gets people's attention and if you have an ad image that goes along with it, that brings the ad copy to life, people are going to pay attention. Not because it's calling them out, you're actually connecting with them and bonded.

Running ads on Facebook but not sure if you're doing them correctly? Join our free group and start profiting from your ads this week!

Looking for gym classes in Dallas? You demanded and now we're delivering. Starting in September, we're opening our new facility, complete with morning and evening classes, pre-register and claim your spot now!

As you can see these ads not only call out the person that I'm looking to attract, but it's also bringing up something they've looked for, something they're experiencing, and I'm providing a solution.

Remember, you want to bring message congruency to the landing page. Make sure that whatever copy you put into your ad is consistent with what the offer is on your landing page. If there is consistency, you are more than likely going to have a high converting offer. You can also have the benefit or desired outcome in the ad copy be the exact same on your landing page.

Lastly, social proof, probably one of the best types of ad copy is giving people the proof, showing the numbers. If you're getting great reviews or testimonials with your product or service, use them to your advantage. People are more likely to believe your ad if they see that what you're offering has worked for others. Having those types of elements in your ad copy, whether it's just one or all, is what brings the psychology element behind your ad creations. Think of Dropbox for example, did you go about looking for it? Or did you want to share a file with a friend and they recommended it to you?

Focus a lot of your time on developing the right type of ad copy, whilst coming up with multiple variations. If you decide to create ads, whether it's two, four, or even six versions of it; consider using one of each of these examples as a version of your ad.

Psychology of Ad Images

When creating your ad images, they must be distinctive, from the patterns and the background to the contrasting colors. Take your time with this, make it look beautiful, it has to make sense from a design standpoint. Do not use a green background with a pink image, use obnoxiously loud colors, or arrows, just for the sake of grabbing someone's attention. There was a time when that was a thing, but it does not work anymore, on Facebook at least. What you can add to your image is a call-to-action (remember no more than 20% text). If the only text on your image has is a call-to-action you'll get an increase in click-through rate.

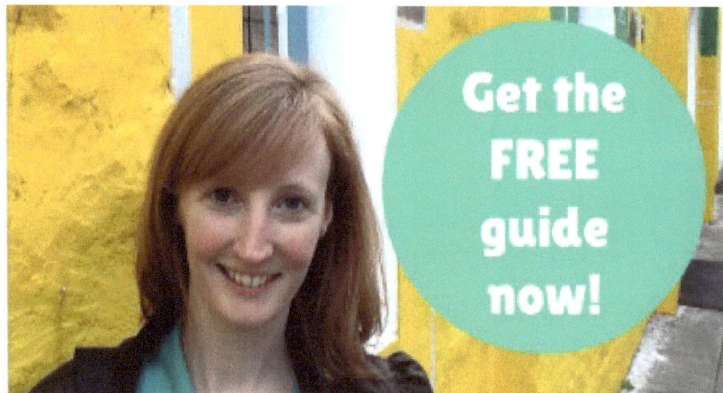

In the above example, it's obvious that there is a free guide of some sort. If the call-to-action was not there, then someone just scrolling through might not stop and look at the ad further.

Side note: If possible, use a human face. Psychologically, when we see a face, we are automatically triggered to feel something or empathize with that person. It helps us feel connected. Faces can add a human touch to your ad, which triggers emotion.

There's a lot of ways that you can incorporate these different sales messages and calls to action that get people's attention when browsing through the news feed. There are articles around the web that talk about one specific color converting better than the rest. There's also a lot of articles that split test all sorts of color variations. To be honest though, it may be true for some sites, but it may not be necessarily true for yours. The same goes for your ad images. I've personally found that images that blend in with Facebook tend to get the most clicks. Those images that contain white, gray, and blue generate more clicks because of that psychology, the user is already attracted to those colors every time they log into their account. It blends in and because it blends in, people are more susceptible to clicking the image.

If you're branding your ads consider your options, personal branding vs. corporate branding. If you want to incorporate your personal brand, whether it's just a picture of yourself or maybe you have a logo or a company brand. You could split test those variations and see which ones perform better. You can also use the editorial look, like a magazine or something that looks like it would come out of a really fancy publication. Your logo can be centered, in the bottom left, or the bottom right, you have options. Once again, one of the best forms of ads are social proof. Anytime you can show numbers in your ad, like 200% ROI on this, 400% increase using this strategy, etc. Of course, remember, you can only have up to 20% text, but if you could showcase an upward trending graph or something along those lines that relate to the solution you are offering to the audience, that will grab someone's attention. Don't go too crazy with it though. You don't have to use super bright colors. You don't have to use anything with bright red arrows or anything like that. Simply create nice, beautiful images, that grab people's attention using any of the things that I just mentioned.

Keep your ads cohesive, keep it consistent, and just make it simple for someone to click. If your content matches what is on the landing page and targeted to the right people, they will click your image.

If you're unable to get your ad images done from an in-house designer, you can go to Fiverr.com and get a couple images done for just 5 dollars apiece. Some of the providers on Fiverr will provide you with more than just one images as well sometimes 3, 4, or 5, done at one time and will cost you no more than 5 dollars. You can also use upwork.com to find a couple of contractors that are graphic designers. Lastly, if you decide you want to create ads on your own, you can always use canva.com, which actually has a prebuilt Facebook ad template size; so that all you have to do is incorporate the images you want into that template and voila, you have a Facebook ad of your own.

Start, Grow, Scale

How Campaigns Work

There are two ways that you can go about creating your campaigns; you can go to the ads manager, click create ad, and follow the instructions there or you can open up power editor and go through those instructions.

Let's just keep this simple for now so you can understand the premise behind the campaign. When you're choosing your campaign, you want to make sure that you are choosing the correct objective. That does not mean that you cannot try an objective and have a second layer of an objective, meaning let's say your main objective is to get as many clicks to your site as possible. Then you're going to create a clicks to website campaign, but your secondary objective may be to gather leads. You'd want to make sure you're tracking your entire clicks campaign by conversions.

If you're looking for just website conversions, you want to make sure that your campaign is focusing on those conversion factors, whether it's registrations, leads, or checkouts. Then you're going to choose, increase conversions on your website. If your goal is to get more awareness to a post, you're going to click boost your post. What you want to make sure is that you have a clear objective in mind when you are creating a campaign.

Bidding Strategies

Facebook gives you a number of ways that you can bid on the interests or the ad sets that you've created, but they can be confusing. For that reason, I'm going to walk you through the exact way I bid on the majority of my campaigns. If you are creating, for example, a page likes campaign, clicks to website campaign, or website conversions campaign; they use different lingo to explain whether or not you are manually bidding versus using automatic bidding. Let's look at the process.

Optimization for Ad Delivery ⓘ **Link Clicks** ▼

Bid Amount ⓘ • **Automatic** - Let Facebook set the bid that helps you get the most link clicks at the best price.
Manual - Enter a bid based on what link clicks are worth to you.

When You Get Charged ⓘ Impression
• **Link Click (CPC)**

I've set up a clicks to website campaign. As you can see, it's currently set to optimize for link clicks. The other options you can optimize for are impressions and daily unique reach. The reason why I typically choose the recommended, link clicks model is because I'm allowing Facebook to do the bidding and the optimizing for me.

If I decided that I wanted to pay a certain price instead of getting more link clicks at the best price, I would select set the bid I'm willing to pay. The strategy with manual bidding model is to outbid my competitors for that audience. Meaning, when my audience is getting targeted with an ad, since I have the highest bid, my ad will take preference over someone else who chose to use the automatic bidding. This is a more expensive approach; however, it can also be effective.

Bid Amount ⓘ **Automatic** - Let Facebook set the bid that helps you get the most link clicks at the best price.
• **Manual** - Enter a bid based on what link clicks are worth to you.

$5.00   per link click

Suggested bid: $2.76 USD ($1.99–$4.26)

AARON C. ST. HILAIRE

For instance, with this campaign, the suggested bid per link click is $2.76 with an average anywhere from $1.99-$4.26. Since I want to outbid my competitors, I set my bid at $5.00, which is way above the average bid price. Realize this though, just because my bid is set at $5.00 per link click, does not mean that I will actually be paying that price. I'm only going to be paying higher than the highest bidder.

However, the only time I really set a manual bid is after I run a test for 7-14 days. I then go back and look at the average link click cost. If I'm getting clicks for $1.00, I'll set to the bid for $1.05, just so I can outbid my opponent that's paying $1.00. Again, just because I keep the bid at that level does not mean that I'm always going to get link clicks at that amount.

When you optimize for the best price, Facebook delivers more clicks. When you set a manual bid, Facebook has to go out and find the people that are worth that amount and the same thing can go for the other ad types.

Whenever I'm getting great link clicks or conversions automatic, I leave it alone. I don't want to manipulate what Facebook is giving me. I don't have a problem letting them determine what's best for my campaign. However, on the back end, I'm tracking all the data to make sure the people coming through my sales funnel are converting.

Same goes for page likes. You can optimize for the page likes, you can optimize for the clicks, and so on and so forth. Just choose the objective that you're going to optimize for and then you decide on the pricing, either automatic or manual. In my opinion, you should start with automatic, after you have run ads for some time or you know your market well enough, then you could set it to manual. Otherwise, you're good to go.

Front End Advertising

It's time to get the essentials of campaign set-up down, that way when you run your ads, they'll be segmented by interests. We want to make it as simple as possible for us to tell what is working and what is not. The first step is to open up Power Editor and create your campaign.

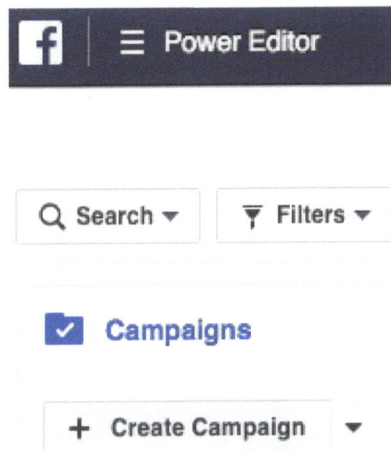

After that, we'll choose our campaign name, objective, ad set name, and ad name. In this case we're going to do the objective of clicks to website, we'll just label our campaign "test." What I typically do is put what type and I'll stick with the example of Pilates classes. For ad sets, let's segment by interests, we'll know exactly what interests when we're deeper in the creation process. For now, we'll use "Interests -." The ad names are simply going to be numbers, so I'll use "Ad 1," and click create.

Create New Campaign ⇕

Campaign Name	Test - Pilates Class
Buying Type	Auction ⇕
Campaign Objective	▸ Traffic ▾

Create New Ad Set ⇕

Ad Set Name	Interests -

Create New Ad ⇕

Ad Name	Ad 1

Creating 1 campaign, 1 ad set and 1 ad

Cancel   Create

Now that our campaign is created, we're going to go into our ad sets.

☑ Campaigns   1 selected ⊗   ⊞ Ad Sets   1 selected ⊗   ▭ Ads   1 selected ⊗

With our ad set selected, we're going to click the edit button.

➕ Create Ad Set ▾   ⊕ Duplicate ▾   ✏ Edit   Quick Edits ▾

Summary

✓	Ad Set Name			Status	Delivery
☑	Interests -		⬆	🔵	○ In Draft

The ad set menu will open up and you can choose your placements, which I will leave as automatic. You can set your budget, which I'll set for $5.00/day. Then, we're simply going to segment our Pilates interests. For all of these ad sets, I'll be targeting women between the ages of 25-54. For this specific ad set, I will target the interest, Pilates Anytime.

Age ⓘ	25 ▼	-	54 ▼		
Gender ⓘ	All	Men	**Women**		

Languages ⓘ	English (All)	×
	Enter a language...	

Detailed Targeting ⓘ INCLUDE people who match at least ONE of the following ⓘ

Interests > Additional Interests

Pilates Anytime

Add demographics, interests or behaviors | **Suggestions** | **Browse**

Now I can plug in my ad set name, Interests - Pilates Anytime and save the changes.

Ad Set Name   Interests - Pilates Anytime

After the changes are saved, we'll be back on the ad set page and from here we can duplicate our ad set to the original campaign and make 4 copies. Then, simply go in, leave everything the same, except the interest. We change the interest to segment them and test which interests are working better than others. When you're done you should have the same amount of ad sets as you have interests and they should be segmented by name.

Ad Set Name

Interests - Revista Pilates

Interests - Physio Pilates

Interests - Pilates Style

Interests - Pilates Anytime

Now that everything is organized in a fashion that is easy to understand, we've completed the basic ad set set-up.

We can now go into the ad level. It will be the same process as the ad set, if you want to create different ads for the different interests.

Let's edit Ad 1 which we made when we first created our campaign. After that, you want to choose the fan page and if you're utilizing Instagram placement, the Instagram account as well.

Destination

Facebook Page ⓘ

Choose a Facebook Page to represent your business in News Feed. Your ad will link to your site, but it will show as coming from your Facebook Page.

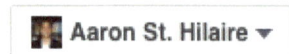

Aaron St. Hilaire ▼

or **Don't Connect a Facebook Page** (will disable News Feed ads).

Instagram Account ⓘ

Select an Instagram account to represent your business in your Instagram ad. Manage your available Instagram accounts in Business Manager.

Use the selected Facebook Page ▼

With that, we're ready to go about creating our ad. You have a number of options to choose from, you can create a new ad with one image, multiple images, a carousel, collection, or full screen canvas. You can do all of the above with images or with video. What I like to do is create a post on my page for the ad first, that way I can keep the social proof (likes, comments, shares) throughout all of my ads. I recommend you do that as well, because you can create a post that looks exactly like an ad.

Once the ad image or video is selected, you can then get into writing the copy. When you're done, it should look something like this.

Aaron St. Hilaire
Sponsored ·

Do you love Pilates, but can never find the time to make it to the gym?

With our online training, we bring the gym to YOU.

Now you can do the workouts you love from the comfort of your home.

To sweeten the deal, we're giving 75% off to the first 25 people who want to access our training now!

Get 75% Off Now!
PilatesTraining.com

Learn More

If you've been practicing along, you would have noticed that Facebook provides you all of the text areas and updates in real-time. You can see how your text looks in your headline, website link, description, etc. Also notice, I used some image psychology, with the face being the focal point. I've also positioned the 75% off to look like the woman is pointing at it. It is an eye-catching image. I've added scarcity to the ad copy as well. These are all things that encourages the user to act on the offer now.

Now that we've got our first ad, inside of our first ad sets, inside of our first campaign, all we've got to do is duplicate them and change whatever is necessary if we have to develop more ads.

That is how you do your basic campaign set-up. You do this numerous times for each ad set, different placements, demographics, interests, etc. As you continue to practice and do this more, it gets a lot easier.

Custom Audiences and Retargeting

Setting up custom audiences for your retargeting is actually very simple to do. The most difficult part is figuring out where to place your pixels, versus the actual set-up. First, in your ads account, navigate to your menu, and select Pixels. Facebook gives you a master pixel and you can find it under actions, you could just view your pixel and everything is there.

The basic use of the pixel is to simply gather data for the custom audiences. You just need to install the pixel on all of the pages that you plan to capture traffic. The best place to paste the pixel code is in the header of your pages. The instructions are provided when you open the pixel in the view pixel code section.

Once you do that you can use the menu to navigate to audiences. In there you want to click create audience, custom audience, then click website traffic.

Create a Custom Audience

How do you want to create this audience?

Reach people who have a relationship with your business, whether they are existing customers or people who have interacted with your business on Facebook or other platforms.

Customer File

Use a customer file to match your customers with people on Facebook and create an audience from the matches. The data will be hashed prior to upload.

Website Traffic

Create a list of people who visited your website or took specific actions.

App Activity

Create a list of people who launched your app or game, or took specific actions.

Engagement on Facebook

Create a list of people who engaged with your content on Facebook.

From there, you can either track anyone who visits your page or any additional parameters. In this case, we're doing just a site-wide pixel for our Pilates funnel and are going to leave it as anyone who visits your website. I'll then set my pixel for 180 days. We then name the audience and click create.

Create a Custom Audience   ✕

☑ Include people who meet ANY of the following criteria:

　● St. Hilaire Marketing ▼

　All website visitors ▼   in the past   180   days ⓘ

　　　　　　　　　　　　　　　　　　🗗 Include More　🗗 Exclude

Audience name Pilates Sales Funnel   30   Show description

Cancel   Back   **Create Audience**

Once you've create your audience, it'll say your audience is too small, because you haven't run any traffic to it yet.

Name	Type	Size	Availability
Pilates Sales Funnel	Custom Audience Website	--	● Audience too small ⓘ

The only way to build this audience up is to run traffic to your ads. Let's say we did run traffic to it and have built up the audience. We would go back to the power editor, go into the Pilates Class campaign, and create a new ad set. Navigating down to the audience, we can select the custom audience we created.

Custom Audiences ⓘ

Website
　Pilates Sales Funnel

Add Custom Audiences or Lookalike Audiences

This allows us to retarget those individuals who have visited our Pilates training website. That's why we're creating a different ad set and we want to set up a different ad as well. Something that lets them know, "hey, you've visited our website, but haven't taken us up on our offer, there's only a few spots left." Something like that to simply remind them that they were interested before.

Remember, your custom audience pixel has to be installed on the header of each of the pages you want to gather traffic from. Make sure that the audience name is specific, so you know exactly where they are coming from. Anytime you want to exclude a person from an audience you simply need to add the pixel that comes after someone takes an action. If they opt-in with their email and get to the sales page, but do not check out, you wouldn't send them a retargeting ad to the opt-in page again. You'd send them to the sales page. Again, it may be confusing, but if you actually practice this it is much easier than just reading it.

That's the basics of retargeting with custom audiences in order for you to optimize your ads and maximize the potential of bringing people back to your website.

Lookalike Audiences

The purpose of lookalike audiences is to create audiences that are most similar, if not almost identical, to whomever you have captured via a custom audience pixel, a conversion pixel, or an email list. Those are the primary ways that I create lookalikes. Just like when you created a custom audience, you can create a lookalike audience by navigating to the audience's tab, click create new audience, and selecting lookalike audience.

For example, let's say I want to do a page likes campaign. I can create a lookalike audience of people who already like my fan page. That way I don't have to waste any time targeting specific interests because Facebook will match those people up for me.

Create a Lookalike Audience

Find new people on Facebook who are similar to your existing audiences. Learn More

Source · Aaron St. Hilaire

Create new ▾

Location · Countries > North America

United States

Search for countries or regions to target · Browse

Audience Size · 2.1M

0   1   2   3   4   5   6   7   8   9   10   % of countries

Resulting audiences · Estimated reach

Lookalike (US, 1%) - Aaron St. Hilaire · 2,120,000 people

In the image above, I selected my fan page as the source, I chose the U.S. as the location I want to target, and finally I chose to select the top 1% of people who most look like the people that like my fan page. The result is an audience size of 2.12 million people that I now have the ability to advertise to.

You can literally create lookalikes from anything you want and will typically be of a high relevance score because it is extremely targeted. Maybe you had 20,000 people visit your website in the last 180 days, you can create an audience of 2.1 million that most directly match that 20,000. That has the potential of expanding your customer base and sales with ease. You can also use lookalikes for post engagement, let's say you uploaded a video of you doing your practice, you can create an audience of the people that have watched 50%, 75%, even 95% of your video and then create a lookalike audience. Facebook will then find the people that will likely watch the same lengths or take the same actions. You can do this with your conversion pixels, you can upload your email subscribers and create a lookalike of them. Can you see how powerful that is?

To be aware though, when you create a lookalike audience it can take Facebook about 30 minutes to actually build it up for you.

The same way you would set up a campaign and use the targeting options within the ad set to pinpoint your audience, is the same way you would do it when plugging in your lookalike audiences. Instead of targeting interests, you can simply select your custom or lookalike audiences. What's beautiful about that as well is you can still target interests. For example, I can plug-in the lookalike audience that are most likely to like my page. On top of that, I can add some interests in there that I would want them to have to be sure they're a good fit for my content. In doing that, I can narrow down that lookalike audience and make it even more specific.

Video Advertising Campaign

You can advertise with a video across multiple objectives, the most common is the video views objective. However, you can also create a video for page post engagement, you can do one for website conversions, or even clicks to website. Personally, I stick with video views because I have found it to be the cheapest and the purpose of my advertising is to get the greatest quality of traffic at the cheapest price.

You would set up your video views campaign like you would any campaign. You'd fill in your budget, your schedule, your audience, etc. You can promote it in the mobile news feed, the desktop news feed, the desktop right hand column, etc. What I have found lately is that when you put your video in the right-hand column, you can get some pretty cheap views because people are not used to seeing a video ad in the right-hand column.

Also, when I'm running video ads I tend to only target people who are connected to Wi-Fi. Why? Well for one, people are cautious of how much data they use because nowadays unlimited data isn't unlimited. Secondly, if they're connected to Wi-Fi, they're typically in a comfortable place like their home or work, somewhere where they actually have time to sit and watch our video ad. This is extremely important, especially if your video is longer than a couple of minutes. Someone that is simply using their cell phone data may be more likely to click off of your ad suddenly.

Just like with any other ad, you can choose what you optimize for and how you're pricing your content. You can optimize specifically for video views, from an impression basis, or even a daily unique reach. I like to leave the pricing at, get the most video views at the best price. As you may have noticed throughout most of my ad set set-ups I let Facebook do the work. I allow the campaigns to focus on getting optimized by Facebook.

Essentially though, you're going to go about creating your ad the same way you would create any other ad. You can choose to upload one video, multiple videos, a carousel, etc. You can use an existing post, write copy, add a call-to-action, etc. There is nothing different except the fact that you're using a video instead of an image. You may even be using a similar objective that you have in the past, it does not have to be video views. When I run video ads, I use either video views or page post engagement. I've found those to be the most cost effective and can drive home results. That doesn't mean I wouldn't ever run a link click campaign with a video, it all depends on the offer and strategy. With that, that's how you can go about creating your video based campaigns.

Scaling Your Campaign

This is probably the most important part of your campaign because this is where people tend to blow their budget and campaign by scaling the wrong way. What people do is, when they see an ad winning and doing they're doing 5-10$/day, they then increase to 50-100$/day, which can bust their campaign. Facebook is optimizing your ads based on your budget, so when you increase drastically and suddenly, it just interferes with Facebook's coding and ruins your traffic patterns.

The key to scaling your Facebook ad campaigns is to increase your budget incrementally. A good rule of thumb is to increase it by 50-100% and don't make another increase for at least 3 days while that optimizes. If you start out at 5$/day, increase to 10$/day, then 15$ to 20$/day.

Your sweet spot budget will depend on your audience size. By sweet spot I mean where you're getting the most leads for the best value and your metrics are flowing properly. Basically, if you're paying 100$/day and you're getting leads for 3$, then you increase to 150$/day and your cost per lead goes up to 8$, your sweet spot is at 100$/day and you shouldn't spend more than that for that specific campaign. That's why it's important to scale incrementally.

Another way you can scale is by simply duplicating an ad set. Let's say you're spending $20/day on one ad set and you want to increase your spend on it. You can duplicate it so that everything stays the same and change the budget, this way it looks like a new ad set so the optimization runs better. I wanted to keep this portion short because it is important.

Expert Tactics

Expert Facebook Targeting

Now that you know the most important aspects of setting a campaign and have practiced it for yourself, we can get into more advanced uses of Facebook advertising. I'm going to explain to you how to get very precise audiences. Not all of the features I'm going to show you are available worldwide, some options are only enabled on the advertising accounts in the United States.

Facebook is always updating how targeting works; they've added "and" statements into the search options for example. Which means if you combine certain options together, they narrow down the targeting to a more defined audience. General interest still uses an "or" statement; I love business or books. When you add a behavior or other demographics it uses an "and" statement I love business and I'm a book reader, I love books and I'm a businessman. When you add multiple options within the other demographics, it uses an "and" statement while the options within behaviors use an "or" statement. In the behavior section, you can pick many options as a behavior but it's a lot like interests, so if you have camping and hiking in interests it's going to use an "or." If you're going to advertise a car, you can't have someone who owns a BMW "and" owns a Mercedes, in the behavior section. It's going to say owns BMW "or" owns Mercedes.

It's important to go through and familiarize yourself with all the available options and what they do and we're going to cover quite a few. If you hover over an option, it tells you what type of audience you will get when that option is selected. Whether it's on your behavior, whether it's under demographics, whether it's under the interest, there's always information provided on each option you select.

Typically, you want to start with a general interest and bring your audience down by adding more demographics and/or behaviors. However, some of the behaviors and more demographic options can act as their own general interests. For example, if you want to target someone by their occupation, that comes under the more demographics section. If you only want to target people who have the occupation of being a realtor, you can actually go to occupation or job type, type in realtor, or industries, real estate; and you can target all those people in that category. Of course, it's always going to depend on what you're trying to target. Always check your options thoroughly before you select an option.

When targeting, quickly glance at the description and make sure it's giving you the audience you're going after. Some of the labels used are a bit misleading. The point is to open your mind to all of the possibilities. Consider that as we are going through these advanced segmentation strategies because you need to familiarize yourself with all the different ways that you can break down your demographic information and behaviors, in order to get the best and most qualified traffic from your ads.

Expert Targeting for Physical Products

I have quite a few friends and colleagues that sell physical products via Facebook and I've learned quite a few tactics from them on how they go about creating targeted audiences for their product using Facebook ads. I'm also going to show you exactly what I found from my own tests as a great way to segment all of your interests and/or your options chosen when advertising physical products.

Let's use an example of pet products and services. Target people with a general interest of "pit bull", but narrow it down by adding behaviors of people who purchase dog products.

INCLUDE people who match at least ONE of the following ⓘ

Interests > Additional Interests

Pit bull

Add demographics, interests or behaviors | **Suggestions** | **Browse**

and MUST ALSO match at least ONE of the following ⓘ   ✕

Behaviors > Purchase behavior > Pet products

Dog products

Add demographics, interests or behaviors | **Suggestions** | **Browse**

You can test the various settings to see which ones work best for your specific niche. With this example it can be Rottweilers, Dobermans, it doesn't matter, but we're testing the behavior of someone who made dog product purchases under the pet products category.

There are other related behaviors in this niche as well, so you can set up multiple ad sets targeting the same interest, but choosing a different behavior using the exact same ad. If you are using 3 ads for each ad set, you can use the same 3 ads for each ad set targeting different behaviors in the same interest. That way, you're able to see which of those behaviors has acted as the best converting offer. You can do this exact same format with any other interest and various other behaviors by just switching them around to best suit what it is you're looking to sell.

Let's say you're selling home garden soil, seeds, tools, tutorial guides, anything in relation to home gardening geared towards those home gardeners.

Age ⓘ   25 ▾   -   54 ▾

Gender ⓘ   All   Men   **Women**

Languages ⓘ   [Enter a language...]

Detailed Targeting ⓘ   INCLUDE people who match at least ONE of the following ⓘ

Interests > Hobbies and activities > Home and garden
Gardening

Add demographics, interests or behaviors | **Suggestions**   **Browse**

and MUST ALSO match at least ONE of the following ⓘ   ✕

Demographics > Parents > Moms
Stay-at-home moms

Add demographics, interests or behaviors | **Suggestions**   **Browse**

and MUST ALSO match at least ONE of the following ⓘ   ✕

Behaviors > Purchase behavior > Buyer profiles
DIYers

Add demographics, interests or behaviors | **Suggestions**   **Browse**

According to the audience insight tool, a lot of the people who are into home gardening or gardening happened to be women who are stay-at-home moms. The target audience in this case would be stay-at-home moms, who have a strong DIY (Do It Yourself) behavior. With that being said I set the age of 25 to 54 to allow myself a large enough segment of data and then I chose the interest as gardening. After that I narrowed down to the stay-at-home mom demographic and further narrowed the audience down by adding DIYers from the buyer profile purchase behavior. Now I have the most targeted demographic for any product I'm looking to sell in that space because it fits the profile of the person I see buying home gardening products.

Let's look at one more example on selling organic or natural foods. We're going to target fit and big city moms, who like the general interest of organic food, and show behaviors of buying natural and organic food.

Detailed Targeting ⓘ   INCLUDE people who match at least ONE of the following ⓘ

> Interests > Food and drink > Food
>
> **Organic food**
>
> Add demographics, interests or behaviors   **Suggestions**   **Browse**

and MUST ALSO match at least ONE of the following ⓘ   ✕

> Demographics > Parents > Moms
>
> **Big-city moms**
>
> **Fit moms**
>
> Add demographics, interests or behaviors   **Suggestions**   **Browse**

and MUST ALSO match at least ONE of the following ⓘ   ✕

> Behaviors > Purchase behavior > Food and drink > Health food
>
> **Natural and organics**
>
> Add demographics, interests or behaviors   **Suggestions**   **Browse**

Why fit moms and big city moms? When doing research in the audience insight tool, I found that a lot of the audience that buys organic and natural food happens to be women, a lot of them happen to be fit moms or big city moms, but at the same time focus a lot of their attention on their health. The interest of organic food is very broad, but what I found under behaviors is the golden nugget, under the food and drink purchase behavior, there's actually a section with health food that focuses on natural and organic.

Obviously, I could sell to these moms, organic or natural related products. Whether it's a specific food item or something about organic and natural food. It can even be a book. It's just a matter of what they're most interested in and that's the demographic that fits that profile.

I hope you understand why I'd go about looking into the behaviors than in the interests and how it all ties together in finding the right buyer profile for a physical product.

Expert Targeting for Local Businesses

Local businesses, in my opinion, need access to the information in this book. Being that small businesses have an extremely high failure rate, it's important that they take advantage of the best marketing platform that is available to them, Facebook. Let me repeat, local businesses can thrive from this information.

Even though you might be selling services instead of physical products for local clients, you still need to put your ads in front of the right people. Do note though, these audiences will be much smaller, depending on the size of the city you target. If you live in a really small city, these settings might make your audience too small to use.

Let's say you're someone that does Facebook, Google, or other social media marketing, and want to do some lead generation for yourself. You can target people who own or manage a small business Facebook page. To filter with this setting, just go to behavior, digital activities and then small business page owners.

INCLUDE people who match at least ONE of the following ⓘ

Behaviors > Digital activities

Small business owners

Add demographics, interests or behaviors | **Suggestions** | **Browse**

These are all the people who own or run a Facebook page and classify as a small business. It makes it easy, just target them all with an ad talking about how you can help them increase their business.

If you want to find a local chiropractor who already has a Facebook page simply enter chiropractor as the job title under demographics, work, job titles. The next piece of data you can target is under purchase behavior, business marketing.

Demographics > Work > Job Titles

Chiropractor

Add demographics, interests or behaviors | **Suggestions** | **Browse**

and MUST ALSO match at least ONE of the following ⓘ   ✕

Behaviors > Purchase behavior > Business purchases

Business marketing

Add demographics, interests or behaviors | **Suggestions** | **Browse**

Now, you've found people who are chiropractor's or classified as a chiropractor and are looking for business marketing to grow their business. That's how you can find some local clients because you're going after the interests that are more susceptible to buying marketing from you, since you have the services they are looking for.

Another example:

Let's say you own a car dealership in Houston, it's a luxury dealership that sells Lexus's, Range Rovers, Porsche's, etc. Now we want to make sure we target those people that have enough money to purchase a car from your dealership. Targeting an income level, $125,000+, gives you a more targeted audience, to an end user that can afford your vehicles.

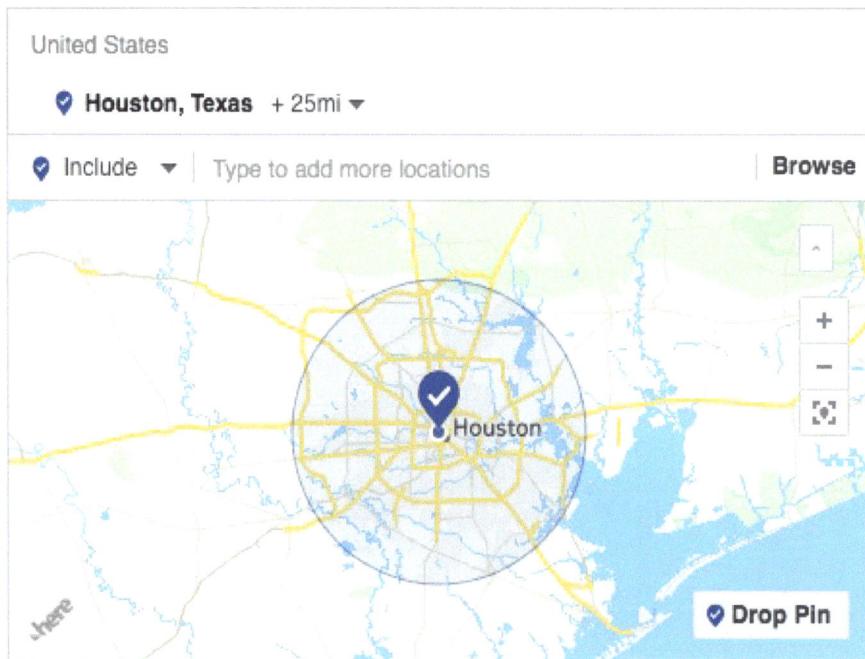

Demographics > Financial > Income

5. $125,000 - $149,999

6. $150,000 - $249,999

7. $250,000 - $349,999

8. $350,000 - $499,999

9. Over $500,000

Add demographics, interests or behaviors | Suggestions | Browse

Narrow Audience

For this particular campaign, I targeted Houston +25 mile radius, with anyone with an income over $125,000. After clicking the "Narrow Audience" button, I targeted further by pinpointing people in the market for Land Rover's, Lexus's, and Porches' from the behaviors section.

and MUST ALSO match at least ONE of the following ⓘ   ✕

Behaviors > Automotive > New vehicle shoppers (In market) > Make

Land Rover

Lexus

Porsche

Add demographics, interests or behaviors | Suggestions | Browse

Narrow Further

EXCLUDE people who match at least ONE of the following ⓘ   ✕

Add demographics, interests or behaviors | Browse

Audience Size

Your audience is defined.

Specific   Broad

Potential Reach: 52,000 people

Estimated Daily Results
Reach
2,000 - 12,000 (of 41,000)   ⓘ

Link Clicks
57 - 270 (of 600)   ⓘ

The best way to run this campaign would be to do three separate campaigns for each vehicle type. However, together, we've got an audience of 52,000 people that are extremely targeted and could potentially be coming to make a purchase at your dealership. Also in this example, the ad spend was $20/day, with the right message, you could be receiving 57-270 clicks/day that are highly likely to convert into revenue. In fact, that opens up the door to being able to track ROI.

Expert Life Event Targeting

Imagine if you could create campaigns for people on their birthdays, they just got married, they just moved, etc. Well guess what, we have the luxury of creating ads for those moments in people's lives.

In the demographics section of your targeting there's an option for Life events and you can select any of the following options from that list. As you can see in the image below you can choose newlyweds, newly-engaged, birthdays, recently moved, long distance relationship, either away from home or family, etc.

Life Events	New relationship
Anniversary	Newly engaged (1 year)
Away from family	Newly engaged (3 months)
Away from hometown	Newly engaged (6 months)
Birthday	Newlywed (1 year)
Friends of	Newlywed (3 months)
Long distance relationship	Newlywed (6 months)
New job	Recently moved

Imagine seeing an ad, targeting you, because of any of these life events.

Got a new job? Here's some of the finest business attire so you can look sharp at work. (Clothing Ad)

Your anniversary within 30 days? Don't forget to buy your wife that necklace she's been staring at. (Jewelry Ad)

New relationship? Stop by our florist shop to surprise your new boyfriend/girlfriend with some hand-picked roses. (Florist Ad)

The possibilities are endless when it comes to what you can do with these life events, so take advantage of it.

Here's an example of great marketing, specifically for recent and upcoming birthdays. Structuring an ad that targets someone within close range of their birthday can psychological attract someone and make them more apt to purchasing your product or service. You can offer special deals just for that occasion.

You can set up limited time offer deals. When selling any kind of physical product, you can use a special link to give to people with an upcoming birthday. Let's say you're a dentist, you can offer a free teeth cleaning because it's their birthday. This gives you the opportunity to upsell them when they come in for that teeth cleaning, that they only came in to get because you knew it was their birthday.

How about life-changing offers? People usually make life-changing decisions or resolutions around New Years' time and their birthday so if you have an offer that can help change someone's life, putting it in front of them during their birthday week can have a great impact. Example, 50% off meals on your birthday for local restaurants. How about around New Year's? Create an offer around New Year's by asking, "ready to make a change in your life this year, ready to get in that shape in that body always wanted to be? Get a free 30-day trial get the new year started off right, for local gyms.

People who have been recently engaged or married are in the middle of big life transitions, need to move into a new house together, buy a new car, plan their honeymoon, the opportunities are endless.

If you're a wedding planner, you can showcase your wedding packages. Travel agents can broadcast vacation packages offering discounts on hotels, airfare, etc. Party planner can showcase their bachelor and bachelorette packages. That's the power of life events and it's not just about birthdays and anniversaries. It's about being able to take advantage of the fact that these are people that are in the moment looking for something right now.

If you have a product or service that's catered to children, you can target those parents with children in the specific range.

INCLUDE people who match at least ONE of the following ⓘ

Add demographics, interests or ... | **Suggestions** | **Browse**

(0-12 months) New Parents

(01-02 Years) Parents with Toddlers

(03-05 Years) Parents with Preschoolers

(06-08 Years) Parents with Early School Age Children

(08-12 Years) Parents with Preteens

(13-18 Years) Parents with Teenagers

(18-26 Years) Parents with Adult Children

Parents (All)

Clearly, the life event options and various are plentiful. I'm sure you see the power of utilizing them in your business.

Expert Broad Interest Targeting

I want to preface this section by noting that this is not about targeting broad interest like cars, food, etc. The purpose of this section is to help find more options if you're having trouble targeting your ideal customer's like and interests. You need a power list of interests and you can find them by looking up the following specified to your niche: associations, federations societies, foundations, clubs, forums, websites, blogs, magazines, newsletters, authors, Amazon bestseller titles, events, festivals, conferences, competitions, subscriptions, etc.

There are so many options out there and a lot of people don't consider all of these different possible broad targets when they're doing their interest research, they just type in the easiest word that they can think of and just go from there, but if you did a little deeper in the look through these types of categories it can potentially provide a breakthrough in your advertising.

Use Amazon, Google search, Google Keyword Planner, etc. and start typing in some things to get some suggestions. For example, if you're in real estate you can type in real estate associations in Google and find a list of different associations, then see if they come up in Facebook as a potential interest to target.

Take your time when you're doing your research there's no reason to rush. I sometimes spend several hours just looking for interests after we've done client research, it's actually my favorite part. How else are we going to find the best possible interest if we don't take the time? Sometimes your best possible interests aren't the ones we're using on our ads. Do deeper research and use the broad targets I provided to you to find those hidden gems all throughout the Facebook ad platform.

Expert Behavior Assortment

In Facebook, behavior allows you to break down your campaigns to reach people based on an intent. Here's a list of behavior categories that can be broken down into deeper categories.

▾ Behaviors
   ▸ Anniversary
   ▸ Automotive
   ▸ B2B
   ▸ Charitable donations
   ▸ Consumer Classification
   ▸ Digital activities
   ▸ Expats

▸ Financial
▸ Job role
▸ Media
▸ Mobile Device User
▸ Multicultural Affinity
▸ Purchase behavior
▸ Residential profiles
▸ Seasonal and Events
▸ Travel

In this example, I'm selling fitness equipment and I want to make sure that I target people who typically might buy these types of products. Under purchase behavior, I want to target people who buy sports and outdoor products, under that I can target fitness. That way I have people who typically purchase fitness equipment.

To sort out my behaviors, I can create an exact lookalike, but change the purchase behavior from fitness to running, that way I can test and see which behavior has a higher ROI for selling treadmills.

The reason you want to separate these behaviors is to see whether or not the performance of one is greater than the other, just like how you would test specific interests against each other, age groups, gender, etc. It's really that simple, sorting by behaviors can help you go even deeper and find all kinds of new buyer profiles.

Expert Age and Gender Assortment

You can always take your campaigns a step further, by deeper targeting after ad optimization, but also before. It's very simple, if you don't know the age group of your most targeted audience, this is what you've got to do. The same way you'd set up different ads and ad sets for different interest and behaviors, you'd do the same for age. Facebook makes it easy by sorting out the age groups for you and you can sort by ages 18-24, 35-34, 35-44, 45-54, 55-64, and 65+. You can further break these age groups down by sorting them by gender, men or women. Running ads to all of these different groups will give you a clear look on the most targeted buyer. Now, this is not to say other ages aren't buyers, but when you're advertising dollars are on the line, you're going to want to be sure you're crossing your t's and dotting your i's.

Expert Placement Assortment

If you've been following along, you'll notice that targeting is actually pretty simple when you play around with it. I personally love separating my ads by placement. Some ads do better on Facebook than on Instagram or better on desktop than on mobile, and vice versa. In fact, that's two of the main options for device arrangement, mobile or desktop; and there are less options for desktop as you can see from the image below, which makes it simple for you to see which works better for your campaign.

Device Types	Desktop Only ▼		
Platforms ▼	Facebook		
	Feeds		✔
	Instant Articles		Ineligible
	In-Stream Videos		Ineligible
	Right Column		✔
	Suggested Videos		Ineligible
▼	Instagram		Ineligible
	Feed		Ineligible
	Stories		Ineligible
▼	Audience Network		Ineligible
	Native, banner and interstitial		Ineligible
	In-stream videos		Ineligible
	Rewarded videos		Ineligible
	Sponsored Messages		Ineligible

To go deeper though, we'd structure ads on mobile by any of the of the necessary options below.

Device Types	Mobile Only ▼	
Platforms ▼	Facebook	
	Feeds	
	Instant Articles	☐
	In-Stream Videos	Ineligible
	Right Column	Ineligible
	Suggested Videos	Ineligible
▼	Instagram	☐
	Feed	☐
	Stories	☐
▼	Audience Network	☐
	Native, banner and interstitial	☐
	In-stream videos	Ineligible
	Rewarded videos	Ineligible
	Sponsored Messages	Ineligible

It's important to realize that by default, the placement is set to all devices and all of the boxes are checked off. If you're planning to advertise on desktop, mobile, and Instagram for instance, you'd create 3 variations of the exact same ad, all in the same framework.

That concludes the Expert Tactics and the book as a whole. I hope you've enjoyed it as much as I enjoyed creating it. My goal is that you learned something worth more than the value of this book and the business we do together in the future. I appreciate you reading through and practicing along with me, I'm sure you're well on your way to creating profitable Facebook ads like a pro!

Thanks so much!

Think Great,
Aaron St. Hilaire

www.ingramcontent.com/pod-product-compliance
Lightning Source LLC
Chambersburg PA
CBHW041449210326
41599CB00004B/186